ENDANGERED ANIMALS in the ARCTIC

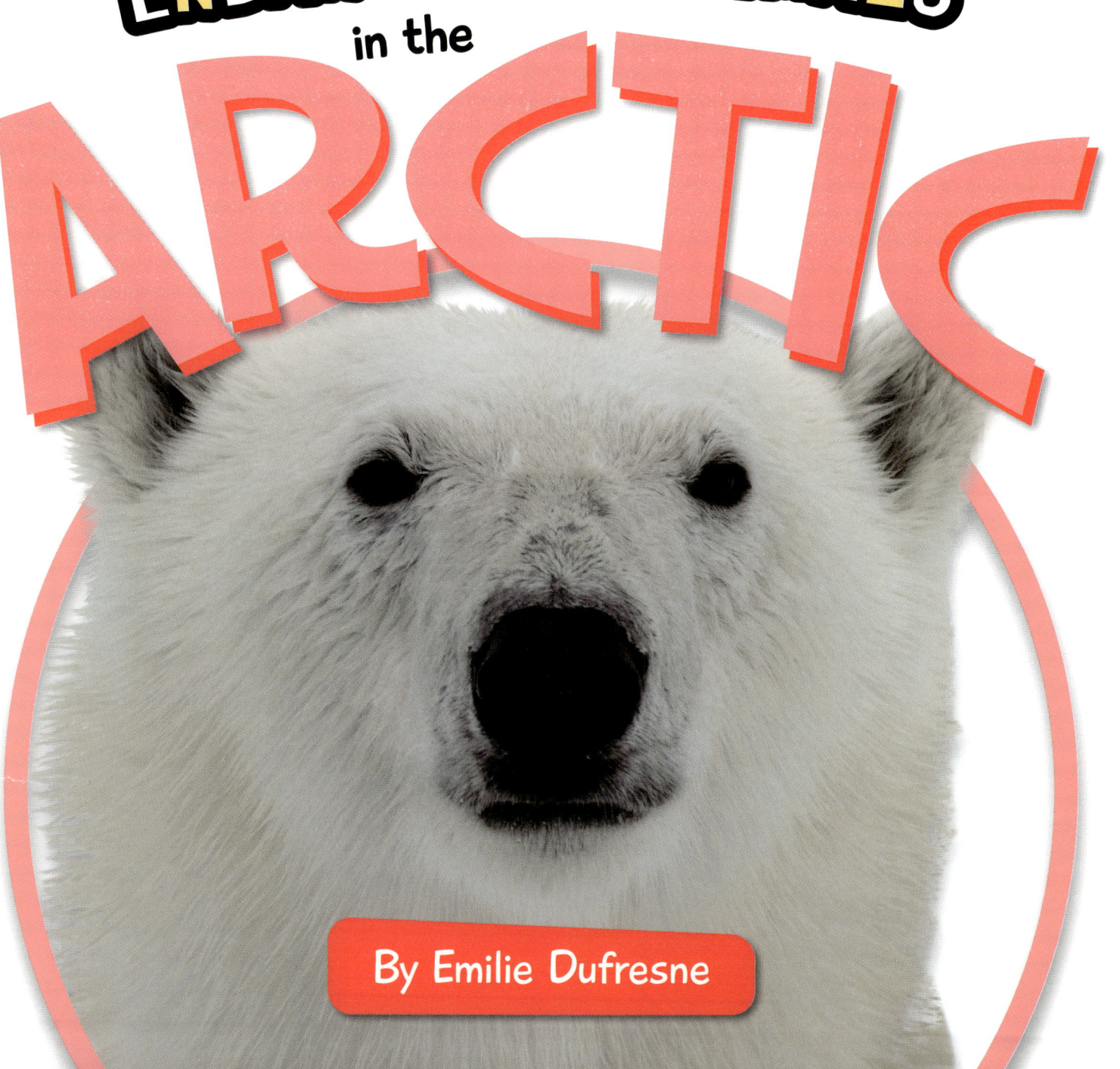

By Emilie Dufresne

BookLife PUBLISHING

©2021
BookLife Publishing Ltd.
King's Lynn
Norfolk PE30 4LS

All rights reserved.
Printed in Malta.

A catalogue record for this book is available from the British Library.

ISBN: 978-1-83927-461-9

Written by:
Emilie Dufresne

Edited by:
Madeline Tyler

Designed by:
Jasmine Pointer

All facts, statistics, web addresses and URLs in this book were verified as valid and accurate at time of writing. No responsibility for any changes to external websites or references can be accepted by either the author or publisher.

PHOTO CREDITS

All images are courtesy of Shutterstock.com, unless otherwise specified. With thanks to Getty Images, Thinkstock Photo and iStockphoto. Cover – murattellioglu, Alexey Seafarer. 4–5 – Ondrej Prosicky, gnohz. 6–7 – Vladimir Melnik. 8–9 – Risto Raunio, ixpert, Andrew Astbury. 10–11 – FloridaStock, barka, Christopher Wood. 12–13 – Jim Cumming, dimcha, MSSA. 14–15 – wildestanimal, Vladimir Melnik. 16–17 – Apple Pho, Chase Dekker, KBel. 18–19 – evgenii mitroshin, evgenii mitroshin. 20–21 – James St. John / CC BY (https://creativecommons.org/licenses/by/2.0), Biodiversity Heritage Library / CC BY (https://creativecommons.org/licenses/by/2.0), Denis Burdin, Tartila. 22–23 – wavebreakmedia, Pixel-Shot, murattellioglu.

Medway Libraries and Archives	
95600000215815	
Askews & Holts	
	£12.99
	HEM

CONTENTS

Page 4   Being Endangered
Page 6   A Closer Look at the Categories
Page 8   The Arctic Habitat
Page 10 Polar Bears
Page 12 Snowy Owls
Page 14 Walruses
Page 16 Blue Whales
Page 18 Reindeer
Page 20 Now Extinct
Page 21 Success Stories
Page 22 Save the Animals!
Page 24 Glossary and Index

Words that look like <u>this</u> can be found in the glossary on page 24.

Being ENDANGERED

When a <u>species</u> of animal is endangered, it means that it is in danger of going extinct. When a species is extinct, it means there are no more of that animal left alive in the world.

Tigers are an endangered species.

There are lots of different reasons that a species might become endangered. If a species loses its habitat, it could become endangered.

Seal

Sea ice

Many Arctic animals are losing parts of the habitats that they rely on, such as sea ice.

5

A Closer Look at the CATEGORIES

Different species are put into different categories depending on how <u>threatened</u> they are.

Data Deficient – Not enough information to know what category the species is in

Least Concern – Currently not in danger of going extinct

Near Threatened – Likely to be threatened soon

Vulnerable – Facing a high <u>risk</u> of extinction in the wild

Always check this website to find the most up-to-date information...

www.iucnredlist.org

Endangered – Facing a very high risk of extinction in the wild

Critically Endangered – Facing extremely high risk of extinction in the wild

Extinct in the Wild – When a species can no longer be found in the wild and only lives in captivity

Extinct – When a species no longer exists in the world

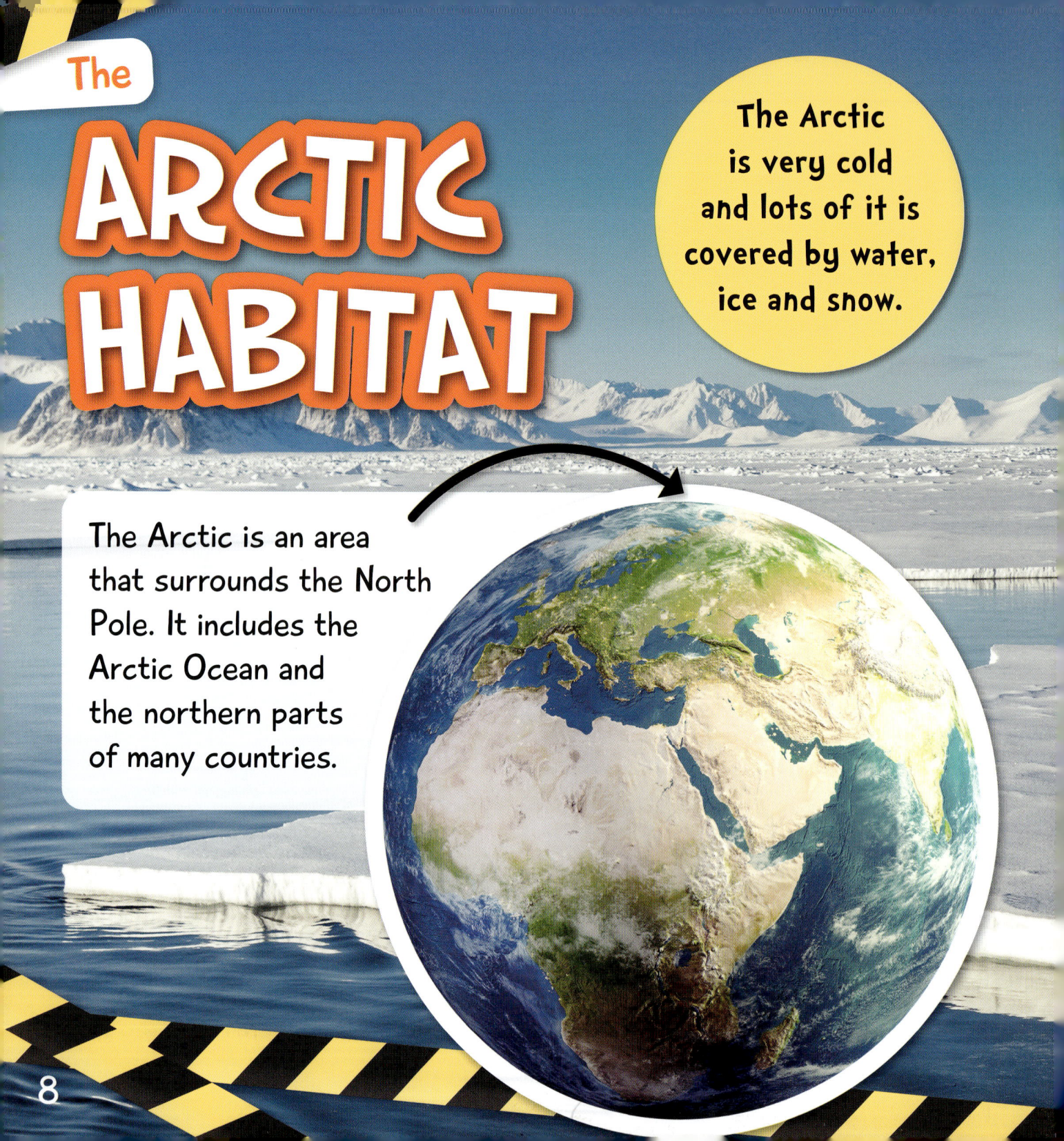

The ARCTIC HABITAT

The Arctic is very cold and lots of it is covered by water, ice and snow.

The Arctic is an area that surrounds the North Pole. It includes the Arctic Ocean and the northern parts of many countries.

Animals that live in the Arctic are adapted to live in its extreme weather. Many of the animals are now facing even more challenges, such as the climate crisis.

This Arctic fox is hidden in the snow by its light-coloured fur.

POLAR BEARS

NAME:
Polar bear

FOUND:
North America and northern Asia

CATEGORY:
Vulnerable

POPULATION:
Between 22,000 and 31,000

Polar bears found

The climate crisis is making the Arctic warmer and melting the sea ice. Polar bears hunt on sea ice and find it difficult to find food without it.

If polar bears don't get enough food, it often means there will be fewer cubs. Polar bear cubs struggle to survive if their mother can't find them enough food.

Polar bear cub

Polar bears have to use lots of extra energy to walk and swim farther to find food.

SNOWY OWLS

The snowy owl population has fallen very low in the past few years. Snowy owls face many threats caused by humans, such as the climate crisis and hunting.

• Snowy owls found

Snowy owls can be killed by vehicles such as cars and aeroplanes. They can also get hurt after becoming tangled in fishing equipment.

NAME:
Snowy owl

FOUND:
North America, northern Europe and northern Asia

CATEGORY:
Vulnerable

POPULATION:
Around 28,000

Snowy owl chick

As the temperature gets warmer because of the climate crisis, it becomes harder for snowy owls to find food for young chicks.

13

WALRUSES

Walruses need sea ice to rest and hunt. Without it, they face many new problems.

NAME:
Walrus

FOUND:
North America, northern Europe and northern Asia

CATEGORY:
Vulnerable

POPULATION:
Around 112,500

Walruses resting on sea ice

Walruses found

More and more sea ice now melts during summer. This means thousands of walruses are forced to head towards land for places to rest.

It can get too crowded if there are too many walruses in one place.

BLUE WHALES

NAME:
Blue whale

FOUND:
Oceans worldwide

CATEGORY:
Endangered

POPULATION:
Between 5,000 and 15,000

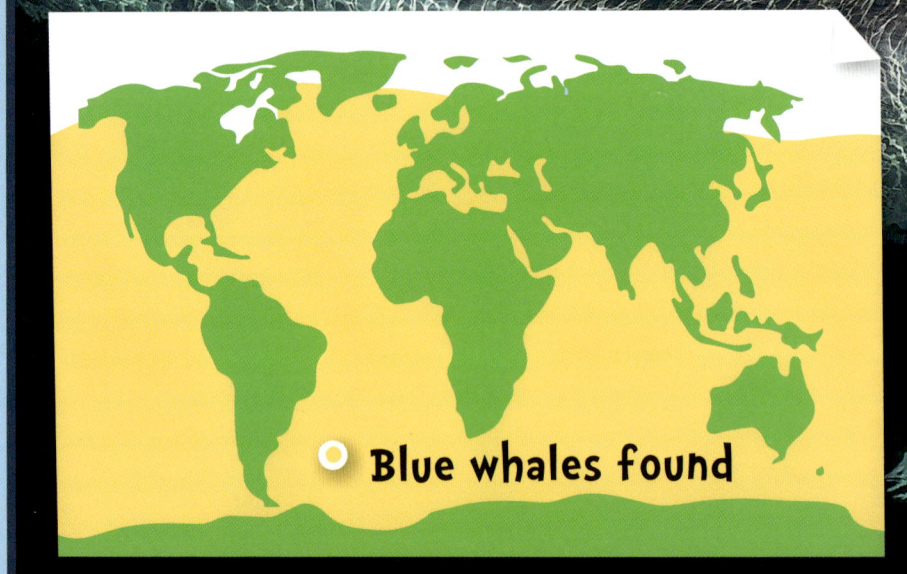

Blue whales found

Blue whales were nearly hunted to extinction in the 1900s. Hunting them is now banned, but the climate crisis means blue whales face new threats.

Blue whales eat tiny sea creatures called krill. Ocean waters are becoming warmer and more <u>acidic</u>, meaning there are fewer krill for the whales to eat.

Krill

Blue whales can also be hit by ships and become tangled in fishing lines.

17

REINDEER

Reindeer are often hunted. This hunting is not checked, so it is hard for scientists to know how much of an effect this has on the reindeer population.

Reindeer found

Warmer weather brings rain instead of snow. The rain freezes and makes it harder for reindeer to find food.

NAME:
Reindeer

FOUND:
North America, northern Europe and northern Asia

CATEGORY:
Vulnerable

POPULATION:
Around 2,800,000

The climate crisis can affect when and where reindeer <u>migrate</u>. Humans have also built on places where reindeer live, making it harder for them to survive.

NOW EXTINCT

Unfortunately, there are many animals across the world that are now extinct. Here are some extinct Arctic animals.

ESKIMO CURLEW

Eskimo curlews lost much of their habitat and were hunted a lot. They haven't been seen for around 50 years and people think they are now extinct.

GREAT AUK

These birds were hunted until they went extinct in the 1800s.

SUCCESS STORIES

Now we know more about <u>conservation</u> and the climate crisis, work can be done to make sure more habitats and animals are looked after.

SAVE OUR PLANET

Lots of work is being done to protect a large area of sea ice in the Arctic known as the Last Ice Area. This will give lots of Arctic animals the habitats they need.

SAVE the ANIMALS!

Driving makes the climate crisis worse, so try to walk or cycle when you can.

22

SPREAD THE WORD!

Tell people about what you know and how they can make a difference. If we all do small things, it can make a big change!

23

GLOSSARY

acidic	contains something that causes damage to some plants and animals
adapted	when an animal or plant has changed over time to suit where it lives
captivity	kept in a zoo or safari park and not in the wild
climate crisis	the very serious problems that are being caused by human action and the changes these actions make in the natural world
conservation	looking after things found in nature, including wildlife
habitat	the natural home in which animals, plants and other living things live
migrate	when animals move from one place to another based on changes in weather, or their food needs
population	the number of animals in a species
rely on	need in order to survive
risk	when there is a chance that something might happen
species	a group of very similar animals or plants that can create young together
threatened	not sure of whether a type of animal or plant will survive

INDEX

climate crisis 9–10, 12–13, 16, 19, 21–22
endangered 4–7, 16
extinction 4, 6–7, 16, 20–21
fishing 13, 17
food 10–11, 13, 19
habitats 5, 8–9, 20–21
migration 19
sea ice 5, 10, 14–15, 21
snow 8–9, 19
temperature 13
vulnerable 6, 10, 13–14, 19